HOUGHTON MIFFLIN

# Hello

INVITATIONS
TO LITERACY

**Houghton Mifflin Company • Boston**

Atlanta • Dallas • Geneva, Illinois • Palo Alto • Princeton

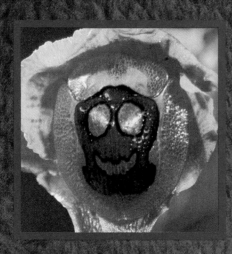

HOUGHTON MIFFLIN

# Hello

**Senior Authors**

J. David Cooper
John J. Pikulski

**Authors**

Kathryn H. Au
Margarita Calderón
Jacqueline C. Comas
Marjorie Y. Lipson
J. Sabrina Mims
Susan E. Page
Sheila W. Valencia
MaryEllen Vogt

**Consultants**

Dolores Malcolm
Tina Saldivar
Shane Templeton

INVITATIONS
TO LITERACY

## Houghton Mifflin Company • Boston

Atlanta • Dallas • Geneva, Illinois • Palo Alto • Princeton

Cover and title page photography by Tim Turner.

Cover illustration from *The Foot Book* by Dr. Seuss. Illustration™ and copyright © 1968 by Dr. Seuss Enterprises, L.P. Reprinted by permission of Random House, Inc.

Acknowledgments appear on page 191.

Printed in the U.S.A.

ISBN 0-395-79494-3

56789-VH-99 98 97

## Getting Started

## Themes

# CONTENTS

The **World** Outside My Door

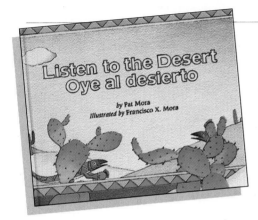

PAPERBACK **PLUS**

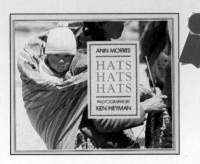

**Hats Hats Hats**
nonfiction by Ann Morris
photos by Ken Heyman
**In the same book . . .**
a map, world stamps and flags, how to make a
paper hat, a song and finger play, and fine art

## CONTENTS

# Get the Giggles

**On Top of Spaghetti**
a song/story
illustrated by Katherine Tillotson
**In the same book . . .**
a song, a diagram, an art activity, and a guessing game

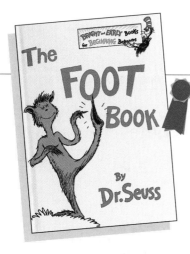

# Meet Patricia and Fredrick McKissack

Patricia and Fredrick McKissack have worked together on almost one hundred books. Most of their books are about people. Mr. and Mrs. McKissack also like to work in their garden. That might be where they got the idea to write about bugs!

# BUGS!

**Bugs.**

Where?

Up here.

One fat red bug.

Bugs. Bugs.

# Where?

Under here.

Two long, skinny, yellow bugs.

Bugs. Bugs. Bugs.

# Where?

Over there.

Three fat, green bugs with two big eyes.

**Bugs. Bugs. Bugs. Bugs.**

# Where?

In here.

Four bugs with four hundred feet.

Bugs. Bugs. Bugs. Bugs. Bugs.

# Where?

Out there.

Five little bugs that fly here and there.

Bugs.  Bugs.

**Lots of bugs.**

# Where?
# Where?

Everywhere!

# Meet Fred Willingham

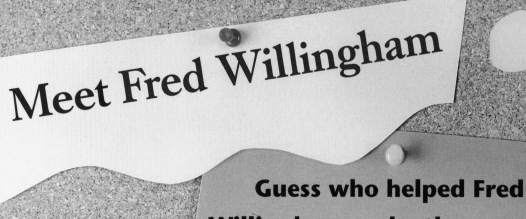

Guess who helped Fred Willingham make the pictures for *Bugs!* It was Desirée, his seven-year-old daughter! She had fun modeling for her dad's drawings.

Mr. Willingham ▷ working on a pastel drawing for *Bugs!*

◁ Mr. Willingham with his daughter

# Bug-a-Boo!

### Make a mask, and pretend you're a bug. You can play hide-and-seek with your friends.

# The World Outside My Door

MY
RIVER

by Shari Halpern

**My River**

*by Shari Halpern*

# Table of Contents

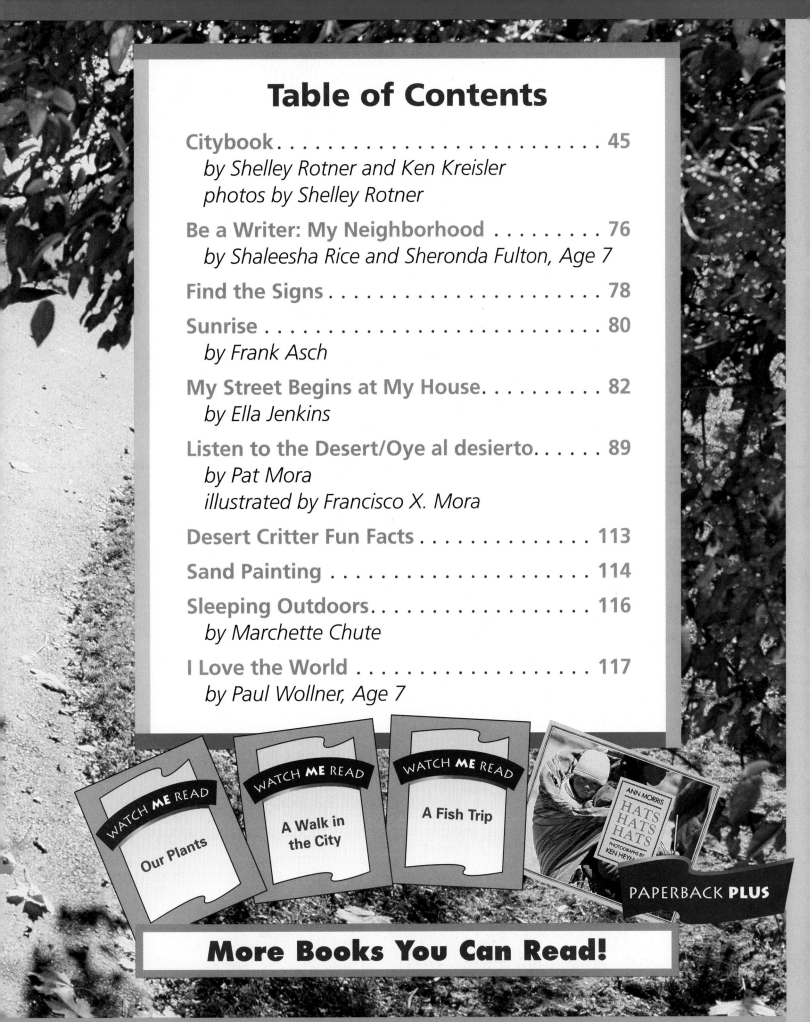

WATCH **ME** READ
Our Plants

WATCH **ME** READ
A Walk in the City

WATCH **ME** READ
A Fish Trip

ANN MORRIS
HATS HATS HATS
PHOTOGRAPHS BY KEN HEYMAN

PAPERBACK **PLUS**

**More Books You Can Read!**

Shelley Rotner often visits New York City with her daughter, Emily. They like to shop, see the museums, and of course, take photographs! Shelley Rotner lives with her family in Massachusetts.

# Meet Shelley Rotner and Ken Kreisler

Ken Kreisler has written four other books with Shelley Rotner. Their latest book is called *Faces*.

Mr. Kreisler also likes to work with his daughter, Samantha. They live in New York City.

Kevin loved to go to the city.

There was so much to see —

lots of people on the go —

riding buses,

taking taxis,

catching trains,

walking, running, roller blading.

Window shopping,

sometimes stopping.

Mimes, music, museums.

Painted walls

and neon signs.

ERASMO'S
LAUNDRY

Long

lines.

65

Fountains, bridges,

statues,                           flags.

So many sights.

So many lights.

# Build a City!

Work in a group. Use boxes or blocks to make buildings. Label each part of your city.

Bank

Police

Store

Post Office

# My Neighborhood

What is your neighborhood like? Shaleesha and Sheronda wanted to write about theirs.

## Shaleesha Rice

William Blackstone Elementary School

Boston, Massachusetts

Shaleesha likes to ride her bike on her neighborhood playground. She's very good at drawing, reading, and doing math. Shaleesha likes to help her friends with their schoolwork, too. Her great-grandmother says that Shaleesha is always happy.

Shaleesha

My neighborhood has beautiful trees.

I have lots of friends to play with.

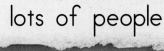
lots of people

a house

## Sharonda Fulton

Roy Clark Elementary
School

Tulsa, Oklahoma

Sharonda likes to play in her neighborhood. She often rides her bike and visits her friend across the street.

Sharonda also walks her dog Buster, but she doesn't go very far because he's too big!

a cat

77

# Find the Signs

A sign is missing from each picture.

Can you find it?

Lemonade 10¢

Wet
Paint

You didn't use all the signs.

Where would you see the others?

# Sunrise

The city YAWNS
And rubs its eyes,
Like baking bread
Begins to rise.

*by Frank Asch*

80

# Sing Along with Ella Jenkins

Here is a picture of Ms. Jenkins with her baritone ukulele.

Ella Jenkins has performed in concerts all over the world. She also teaches music classes called rhythm workshops. There, children share songs, dances, games, and chants from different countries.

# MY STREET
## Begins at My House

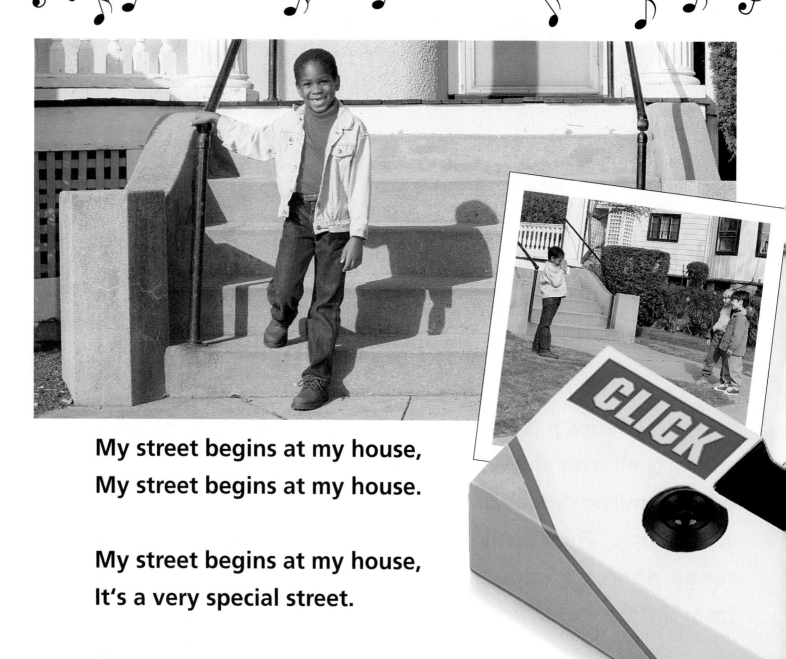

My street begins at my house,
My street begins at my house.

My street begins at my house,
It's a very special street.

On my street things go up and down,
On my street things go round and round.

On my street things go upside down,
It's a very special street.

My street begins at my house,
My street begins at my house.

My street begins at my house,
It's a very special street.

Meet my new friends.

My new house

To Grandma

My New Street

# Meet Pat Mora

Pat Mora grew up in the southwestern United States, where she learned English and Spanish. She says that she can hear the sounds of the desert in both languages. Now Ms. Mora writes books and poetry in both languages, too.

# Meet Francisco X. Mora

Francisco X. Mora grew up in Mexico. He likes to paint flowers, lizards, armadillos, and other things he saw there as a child.

"My paintings are to be enjoyed," he says. "They talk about friendship, joy, and the beauty of nature and life."

Listen to the desert, pon, pon, pon.
Listen to the desert, pon, pon, pon.
Oye al desierto, pon, pon, pon.
Oye al desierto, pon, pon, pon.

Listen to the owl hoot, whoo, whoo, whoo.

Listen to the owl hoot, whoo, whoo, whoo.

¡Oye!  La lechuza, uuu, uuu, uuu.

¡Oye!  La lechuza, uuu, uuu, uuu.

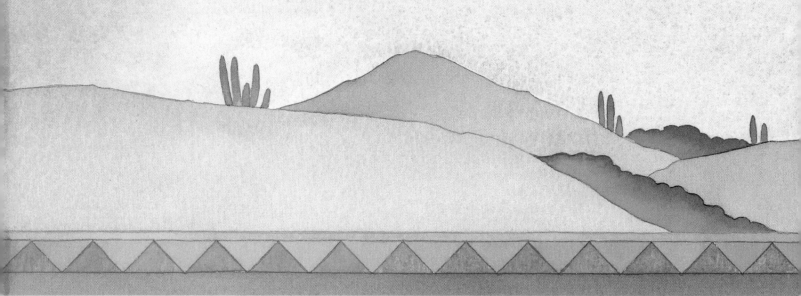

Listen to the toad hop, plop, plop, plop.
Listen to the toad hop, plop, plop, plop.
Oye al sapito, plap, plap, plap.
Oye al sapito, plap, plap, plap.

Listen to the snake hiss, tst-tst-tst, tst-tst-tst.
Listen to the snake hiss, tst-tst-tst, tst-tst-tst.
Silba la culebra, ssst, ssst, ssst.
Silba la culebra, ssst, ssst, ssst.

Listen to the dove say coo, coo, coo.

Listen to the dove say coo, coo, coo.

La paloma arrulla, currucú, currucú, currucú.

La paloma arrulla, currucú, currucú, currucú.

Listen to coyote call, ar-ar-aooo, ar-ar-aooo.
Listen to coyote call, ar-ar-aooo, ar-ar-aooo.
El coyote canta, ahúúú, ahúúú, ahúúú.
El coyote canta, ahúúú, ahúúú, ahúúú.

Listen to the fish eat, puh, puh, puh.
Listen to the fish eat, puh, puh, puh.
¡Oye!  Los pescaditos, plaf, plaf, plaf.
¡Oye!  Los pescaditos, plaf, plaf, plaf.

Listen to the mice say scrrt, scrrt, scrrt.

Listen to the mice say scrrt, scrrt, scrrt.

¡Oye!  Los ratoncitos, criic, criic, criic.

¡Oye!  Los ratoncitos, criic, criic, criic.

Listen to the rain dance, plip, plip, plip.
Listen to the rain dance, plip, plip, plip.
Lluvia baila, baila, plin, plin, plin.
Lluvia baila, baila, plin, plin, plin.

Listen to the wind spin, zoom, zoom, zoom.
Listen to the wind spin, zoom, zoom, zoom.
Oye, zumba el viento, zuum, zuum, zuum.
Oye, zumba el viento, zuum, zuum, zuum.

Listen to the desert, pon, pon, pon.
Listen to the desert, pon, pon, pon.
Oye al desierto, pon, pon, pon.
Oye al desierto, pon, pon, pon.

# Our Guide to Desert Animals

Draw and write about a desert animal. Work in a group. Put your pages together to make a book.

This is a mouse.

scrr-scrrt

# Desert Critter Fun Facts

This dune cricket uses its feet to keep from sinking into the sand.

Camels can go for six days without a drink.

Roadrunners can run five blocks in just one minute!

# Sand Painting

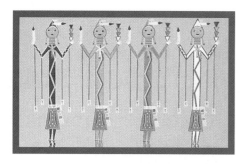  

These Navajo men are making a painting from sand.

# You can draw using sand!

Draw a picture.

Spread glue on one part.

Choose one color. Sprinkle the sand on the glue. Let it dry.

Shake off the extra sand.

Repeat with another color.

# Sleeping Outdoors

Under the dark is a star,

Under the star is a tree,

Under the tree is a blanket,

And under the blanket is me.

*by Marchette Chute*

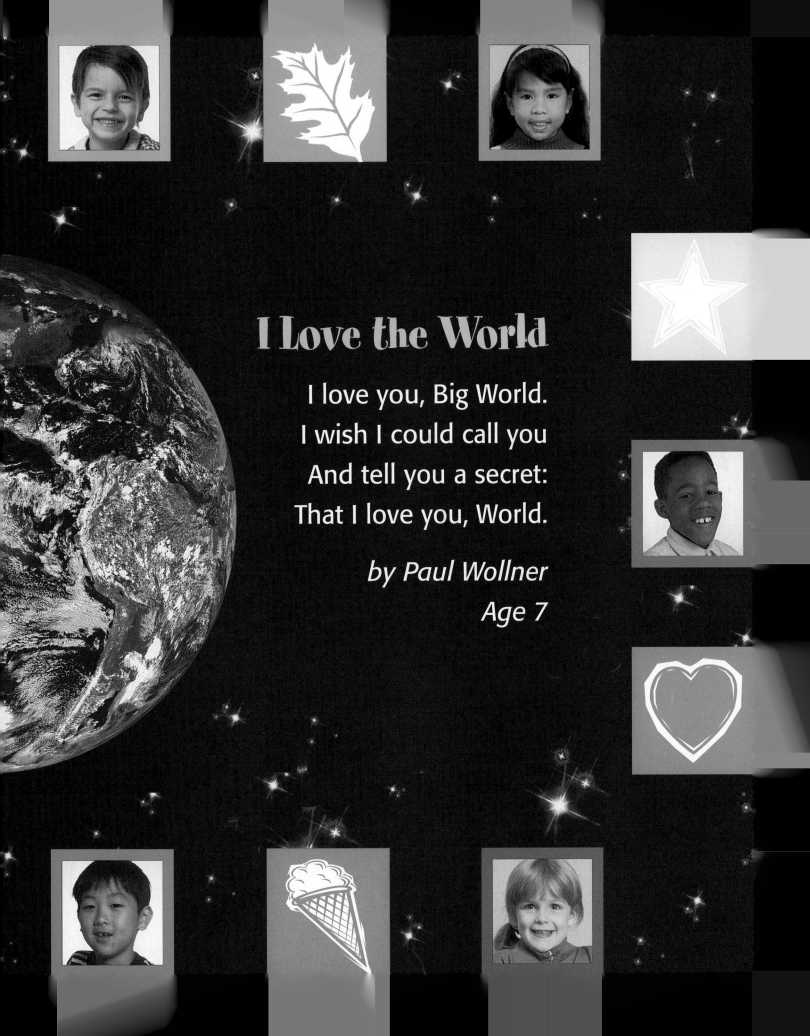

# I Love the World

I love you, Big World.
I wish I could call you
And tell you a secret:
That I love you, World.

*by Paul Wollner*

*Age 7*

# the Giggles

HA
HA

On Top of Spaghetti

On Top of Spaghetti

A Traditional Story and Song
illustrated by
Katherine Tillotson

**On Top of Spaghetti**

*illustrated by*
*Katherine Tillotson*

**BIG** BOOK **PLUS**

# Table of Contents

WATCH **ME** READ

Where IS
My Baby?

WATCH **ME** READ

Fox and
Chick

WATCH **ME** READ

Hank and Lin

Hooray
for Snail!

John Stadler

PAPERBACK **PLUS**

**More Books You Can Read!**

# Meet Dr. Seuss

Dr. Seuss's real name was Theodor Seuss Geisel. He wanted children to have fun reading, so he used easy words and funny rhymes in his stories.

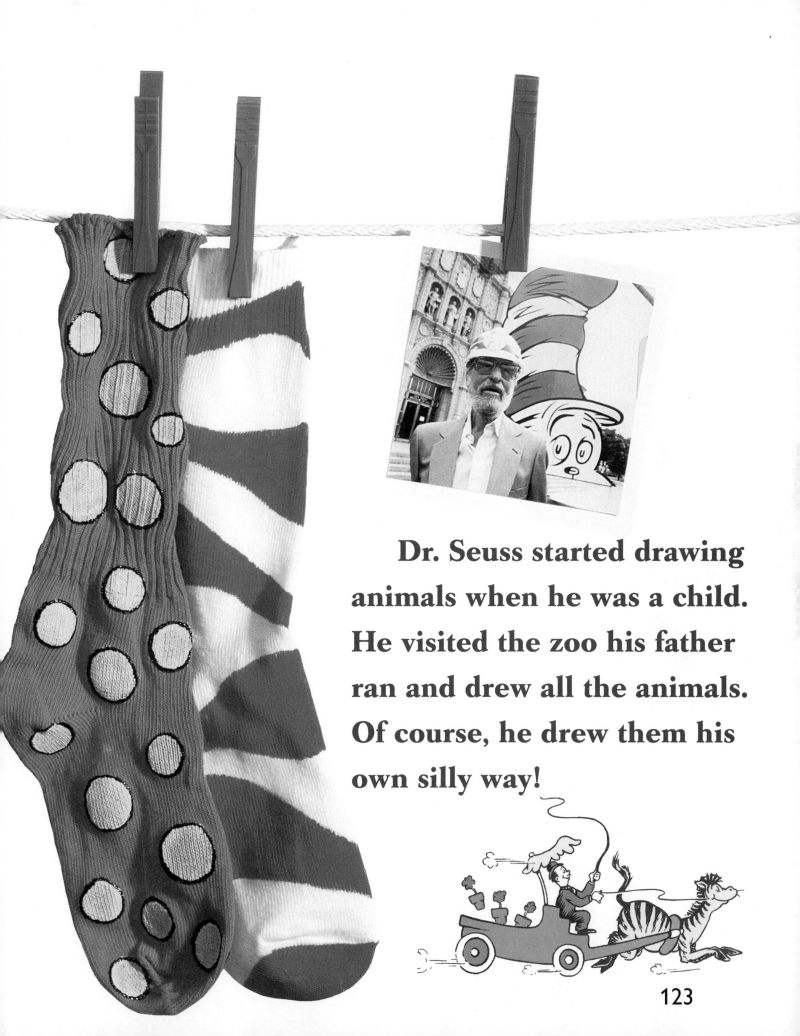

Dr. Seuss started drawing animals when he was a child. He visited the zoo his father ran and drew all the animals. Of course, he drew them his own silly way!

124

Left foot
Left foot

Right foot
Right

Feet in the morning

Feet at night

Left foot

Left foot

Left foot

Right

127

Wet foot

Dry foot

High foot

Low foot

Front feet

Back feet

Red feet

Black feet

Left foot

Right foot

Feet

Feet

Feet

How many, many
feet you meet.

Slow feet

Quick feet

Trick feet

Sick feet

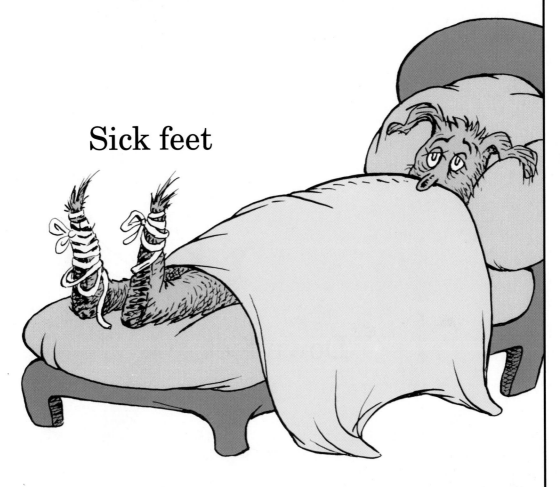

Up feet

Down feet

Here come clown feet.

Small feet

Big feet

Here come pig feet.

His feet

Her feet

Fuzzy fur feet

In the house,
and on the street,

how many, many
feet you meet.

Up in the air feet

Over a chair feet

# More and more feet

Twenty-four feet

Here come
more and more . . . . . . . . . .

. . . . . . . and more feet!

Left foot.          Right foot.

Feet.  Feet.  Feet.

Oh, how many
feet you meet!

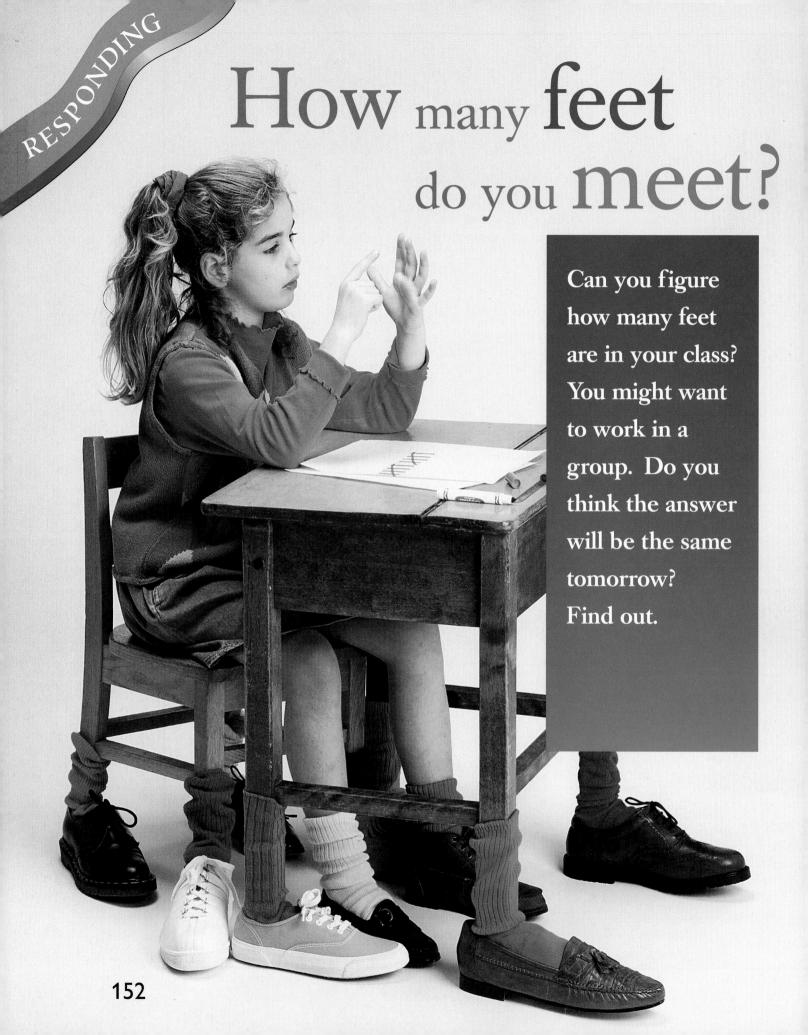

# How many feet do you meet?

Can you figure how many feet are in your class? You might want to work in a group. Do you think the answer will be the same tomorrow? Find out.

152

Knock, Knock, Knock!

WHO'S THERE?

**Knock knock**

Who's there?

**Beets**

Beets who?

**Beets me,  I just forgot my name!**

**Knock knock**

Who's there?

**Ken**

Ken who?

**Ken I come in?  I'm freezing out here!**

154

**Knock knock**
Who's there?
**Ketchup**
Ketchup who?
**Ketchup with
me and I'll tell
you.**

# Can you find the Funny Faces in Funny Places?

156

**Flower**

**Caterpillar**

**Moth**

**Beetle**

# GiggleTime

Do pictures make you giggle? Thuy and Erik wanted to draw silly pictures and write about them.

This clown is funny because it is in outer space, and it is swimming.

## Erik Mitchel Cornelius

John F. Kennedy Elementary School
Green Bay, Wisconsin

Erik enjoys school. He loves to learn. He likes reading and drawing best.

Erik also enjoys sports, especially football and hockey with his friends and brothers.

The cat was growing hair.
The sun was growing hair.
The birds, the butterflies,
and the flowers were growing
hair too.

**Thuy Huynh**
Navy Point Elementary School
Pensacola, Florida

Thuy is a very good student. She likes
math, and she is good in reading, writing,
and drawing. Thuy wants to be a firewoman
when she grows up.

# POEMS AND DRAWINGS
## by Shel Silverstein

SNAP!

She was opening up her umbrella,
She thought it was going to rain,
When we all heard a snap
Like the clap of a trap
And we never have seen her again.

## THE LOST CAT

We can't find the cat,
We don't know where she's at,
Oh, where did she go?
Does anyone know?
Let's ask this walking hat.

Miss Lucy had a baby,
His name was Tiny Tim,

She put him in the bathtub
To see if he could swim.

He drank up all the water,
He ate up all the soap,

He tried to eat the bathtub,
But it wouldn't go down his throat.

Miss Lucy called the doctor,

Miss Lucy called the nurse,

Miss Lucy called the lady
With the alligator purse.

In came the doctor,

In came the nurse,

In came the lady

With the alligator purse.

"Mumps," said the doctor,

"Measles," said the nurse,

"Nonsense!" said the lady
With the alligator purse.

"Penicillin," said the doctor,

"Castor oil," said the nurse,

"Pizza!" said the lady
With the alligator purse.

Out went the doctor,
Out went the nurse,

Out went the lady
With the alligator purse.

# Nadine Bernard Westcott

likes to make her readers laugh. She writes silly stories that show lots of funny things going on at the same time. She often puts cats in her stories. She draws them with silly faces or doing something silly. Can you find a cat in this story?

# Give Them a Call!

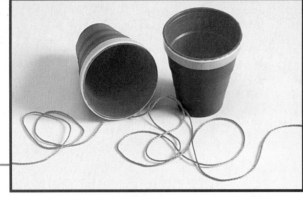

Use string and two cups
to make telephones.
Work with a friend.

Now act out the
phone calls made
in the story.

186

# Bath Time for Calvin

## by Bill Watterson

# She Fell into the Bathtub
## by Jack Prelutsky

She fell into the bathtub,
She fell into the sink,
She fell into the raspberry jam,
And

came

out

pink.

# Shake **My Sillies** Out

Music by
**Raffi**

Gotta **shake**, **shake**, **shake** my sillies out,

Shake, **shake**, **shake** my sillies out,

Shake, **shake**, **shake** my sillies out,

And **wiggle** my waggles away.

Words by
**Bert and
Bonnie
Simpson**

Gotta **jump**, **jump**, **jump** my jiggles out,
**Jump**, **jump**, **jump** my jiggles out,
**Jump**, **jump**, **jump** my sillies out,
And **wiggle** my waggles away.

Gotta **shake**, **shake**, **shake** my sillies out,
**Shake**, **shake**, **shake** my sillies out,
**Shake**, **shake**, **shake** my sillies out,
And **wiggle** my waggles away.

# ACKNOWLEDGMENTS

For each of the selections listed below, grateful acknowledgment is made for permission to excerpt and/or reprint original or copyrighted material, as follows:

**Selections**

*Bugs!,* by Patricia and Fredrick McKissack. Copyright © 1988 by Regensteiner Publishing Enterprises, Inc. Reprinted by permission of Childrens Press.

"Can You Find the Funny Faces in Funny Places?" from the March, Series III issue of *Your Big Backyard* magazine. Copyright © 1984 by The National Wildlife Federation. Reprinted by permission.

*Citybook*, written by Shelley Rotner and Ken Kreisler, illustrated by Shelley Rotner. Text copyright © 1994 by Shelley Rotner and Ken Kreisler. Illustrations copyright © 1994 by Shelley Rotner. Reprinted by permission of Orchard Books.

*The Foot Book,* by Dr. Seuss. Copyright © 1968 by Dr. Seuss. Reprinted by permission of Random House, Inc.

"Knock Knock . . . Who's There?" traditional.

*The Lady with the Alligator Purse*, by Nadine Bernard Westcott. Copyright © 1988 by Nadine Bernard Westcott. Reprinted by permission of Little, Brown & Company.

*Listen to the Desert/Oye al desierto*, by Pat Mora, illustrated by Francisco X. Mora. Text copyright © 1994 by Pat Mora. Illustrations copyright © 1994 by Francisco X. Mora. Reprinted by permission of Clarion Books, a division of Houghton Mifflin Company. All rights reserved.

Comic strip from *Yukon Ho! A Calvin & Hobbs Collection,* by Bill Watterson. Copyright © 1987 by Bill Watterson. Reprinted by permission of Universal Press Syndicate.

**Poetry**

"I Love the World," by Paul Wolner, from *Miracles: Poems by Children of the English-Speaking World*, collected by Richard Lewis. Copyright © 1966 by Richard Lewis. Reprinted by permission of The Touchstone Center, New York.

"The Lost Cat," from *A Light in the Attic,* by Shel Silverstein. Copyright © 1981 by Evil Eye Music, Inc. Reprinted by permission of HarperCollins Children's Books, a division of HarperCollins Publishers.

*My Street Begins at My House*, by Ella Jenkins. Copyright © 1971 by Ella Jenkins, ASCAP. Reprinted by permission of Ell-Bern Publishing.

"Shake My Sillies Out," music by Raffi, words by Raffi and B. & B. Simpson. Copyright © 1977 by Homeland Publishing, a division of Troubadour Records Ltd. Reprinted by permission.

"She Fell into the Bathtub," public domain.

"Sleeping Outdoors," from *Rhymes About Us*, by Marchette Chute. Copyright © 1974 by Marchette Chute. Reprinted by permission of Elizabeth Roach.

"Snap!" from *A Light in the Attic,* by Shel Silverstein. Copyright © 1981 by Evil Eye Music, Inc. Reprinted by permission of HarperCollins Children's Books, a division of HarperCollins Publishers.

"Sunrise," from *City Sandwich*, by Frank Asch. Copyright © 1978 by Frank Asch. Reprinted by permission of Greenwillow Books, a division of William Morrow & Company, Inc.

Special thanks to the following teachers whose students' compositions appear in the Be a Writer features in this level: Sabreen Akbar, William Blackstone Elementary School, Boston, Massachusetts; Leslie Edwards, Ray Clark Elementary School, Tulsa, Oklahoma; Linda Vaile, John F. Kennedy Elementary School, Green Bay, Wisconsin; Ramona Wright, Navy Point Elementary School, Pensacola, Florida.

# CREDITS

**Illustration** **5, 11–37** Fred Willingham; **6, 42** Shari Halpern; **76** Shaleesha Rice; **77** Sheronda Fulton; **80** Mike Reed; **1, 2** (left center), **7, 90–111** Francisco X. Mora; **8, 120** Katherine Tillotson; **9, 121** John Stadler; **8, 122–151** Theodor S. Geisel (Dr. Seuss); **158** Erik Mitchel Cornelius; **159** Thuy Huynh; **160–161** Shel Silverstein; **9, 162–185** Nadine Bernard Westcott; **187** Bill Watterson

**Assignment Photography** **10–11, 38, 76–77, 82** (bottom center), **87** Banta Digital Group; **81** Dan Rest; **88–89, 112** (border), **118–124, 152–155, 162, 164–165, 185–186, 188** Tony Scarpetta; **185** Terry Pommett; **39, 40–43** (background), **2** (top), (right center), **75, 78–79, 82–86, 112, 115, 118–121, 186, 189–190,** Tracey Wheeler

**Photography** **2** Sandved Photography (b) **10** Courtesy of the McKissacks **38** Courtesy of Fred Willingham **40** ©Wolfgang Kaehler/Liason International (mr); ©Chromosohm/Sohm MCMXC11/The Stock Market (l); © 1994 Zefa Germany/The Stock Market (ml); © 1994 Zefa Germany/The Stock Market (m) **44-45** ©Robert Landau/Westlight **44** Courtesy of Ken Kreisler (t); Jose Ramon Garcia/ Courtesy of Shelley Rotner (b) **76** Courtesy of Shaleesa Rice **77** Courtesy of Sheronda Fulton **88** Courtesy of Pat Mora (tl); Courtesy of Francisco X. Mora (br) **113** ©Wolfgang Kaehler/Liason International; Anthony Banister/Natural History Photographic Agency (tl); ©Thomas D. W. Friedman/Photo Researchers (mr); ©Roy Morsch/The Stock Market (bl) **114** Mark Bahti (t,tm,tr); Emil Muench/ Photo Researchers (b) **116** © Photri/The Stock Market **123** Robert Burroughs/Liaison International **156** Lynn Stone (tl) **156** ©Kjell B. Sandved/Sandved Photography (b) **157** ©Kjell B. Sandved/Sandved Photography (tl,bl,br); **157** Larry West (bl) **158** Courtesy of Erik Mitchel Cornelius (mr) **159** Courtesy of Thuy Huynh (ml) **185** Terry Pommett/ Courtesy of Nadine Bernard Westcott (tl) **189** Mario Ruiz/Courtesy of Raffi